Daydreams

Daydreams

~

a book of
poems, stories, and
drawings about life, love, and
the pursuit of happenstance
(via meditation, philosophy,
and friendship)

~

Cole Feldman

Daydreams by Cole Feldman

Copyright © 2017 by Cole Feldman

All rights reserved.

A special thank you to my friends:
Marta, Annie, Alexis, Kiley, Ford, Matthew, Andrew, Kyle and Michael.

www.colefeldman.net

ISBN: 0996360816
ISBN-13: 978-0996360814

For Cat

What goes on four feet in the morning, two feet at noon, and three feet in the evening?

- the Sphinx's riddle to Oedipus

CONTENTS

Part III: Evening

Part I: Morning

Library.

The breath and the force are two things; they are the rocking chair in the library. I sit next to someone I do not know. A whole crowd of people walks by on either side. I am caught between seeing their faces and trying not to. Not reading a book but pretending to.

I rock back and forth. I see the same faces pass by on either side and behind me don't know where they go before I see them again passing in front of me, sometimes different, sometimes the same, sometimes together.

I rock my chair into a swing. At first conscious of knocking into people passing by until accidentally I do, but no physical collision occurs.

I start to swing wider, less conscious about the physical constraints of the library reality, my sensory mental having broken now so vividly from the physical.

I swing in a wide sweeping circle and pass through a mirror on the left side into a crystalline, bright, jagged, reflective oblivion, like the inside of a massive glass snowflake on a sunny day—I really left it all then, in a dream, on a swing that was actually a rocking chair, passing effortlessly through space, but seeming not to.

Library cont.

I pass from the oblivion through the mirror and back into the library, farther up on the left side from where I started. I swing on the same circular course, above the bookshelves and at first worry about kicking over the books on top but then remember being outside of the physical space as my feet and legs pass smoothly through them, so that now I swing quite quick and widely around the whole library of people and books.

At first worrying about all the collisions but soon getting used to not being and so passing through everything as my sensory mind swings but all the time feeling my body to be just sitting in the rocking chair as people pass by.

All inexplicably blissful, I keep swinging until my foot knocks over a book off the top of a bookshelf and I panic as I realize I have been passing through the physical space all this time without worry and so have chartered a circular course on the swing with many impending collisions.

I can feel my physical self in the rocking chair begin to panic and worry about the people walking by looking at me as I expect to crash out of my mental swing and so grab the arms of the rocking chair and wake up out of my daydream.

Wake.

I wake slowly and without urgency until I realize I must grab it quick and reach for my phone to snatch its tail and type it back.

Remember, remember: I say to myself. Write it, write it: only it can't all be written, and some escapes being kept.

But from the dream world some language travels back after wake and I type into my phone, between three and four in the morning, what my dream oracle told me.

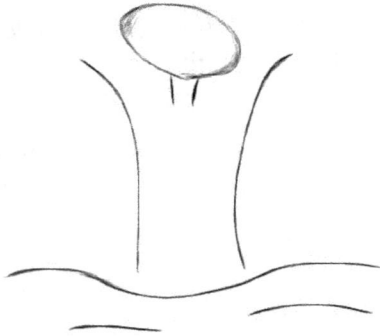

Gun.

My brother and I tiptoe down the building with so many floors where everyone is looking for us except the young kids who are on our side so when they see us creeping down they just shake their heads, smile, and act like they don't see us so the adults won't find out until we get to the basement and my brother has to pack his stuff to leave and that's when she finds us and really starts to yell.

My brother hands me the gun and I run ahead and get in the driver's seat of the car, holding a double long barrel shotgun cracked in half at its waist looking at the gold pristine butts of two shells peeking out of the inside ends of each barrel.

I snap the gun straight hiding the golden shells in front of both silver hammers, pull back the hammers until they click into place, set my finger on the double action trigger and rest the two barrels on the half-open window, waiting for my brother to get out of there.

Starting to wonder what is taking him so long and thinking about how when you hold a gun for the first time with the intention to shoot it at someone, your heart really starts to beat like a tribal drum in your chest and your ears only work on the inside to echo the drum bangs in your hot hollow torso.

Gun cont.

I imagine what it would be like to be shot in the stomach and have that giant hot mess spill out, and wonder what it would be like to die, if this were more than a dream; thinking about how when you die in a dream, wake and begin a new day, just like you die to a day, sleep and begin a new dream.

I stay there, forever, in some sense, gripping that gun just so, as the divide between real and dream dilates and I live a whole lifetime in a blink of sleep.

I wake so dubious of my safe, dark bedroom and sleepy body and wonder where my dream life has gone only to forget it and wake up to use the bathroom and re-enter my real life—but still wondering if I might live a whole life (and death) in a dream.

Dream.

There are two worlds
on either side of the line
that divides sleep and wake
in those early morning hours
when you cannot tell which is which,
figments drift over to the real bedroom
and the clock from your nightstand
dances in between dreams.

In a half-reality
the dream borrows
from the real
to form a mirage
right on the line
between the two.

In and out of sleep,
dry under warm sheets
each borrows from the other
and the storm going on
outside my real window
dances into the dream.

In the nighttime
I dream so many dreams
that I don't remember,
and think in the morning:

Dream cont.

how many lifetimes
have I lived
before this one?

Day.

We wake up and make breakfast. In the morning it is clear and sunny. At night it is dark and foggy. We eat. We are tired. On our way home, I think I am needing nothing. When my friend leaves I sit on the edge of my bed and wonder what to do.

I am tired but not sleepy. I look at some things. I read a little. I live a whole lifetime in a day. Accidentally, I fall asleep. I wake new and with refreshed needs. I get out of bed curious about my new life and the change of scenery.

Age.

My child mind,
like my child body,
used to run all over
—fast as it could,
in and out of smaller spaces
and up and down big spaces.

Now my older mind,
like my older body,
conserves its energy
—sitting on the shore
with binoculars
watching ships,
waiting for one
with treasure
and worth the swim out
before I neatly undress
and dive in.

But some ships keep their treasure beneath the deck, and these are the ships I boarded when I was young.

When I was younger, I created, because nothing was too surreal to inhibit my chasing after it. Now, I conserve my energy and err toward real pursuits.

Age cont.

You become an adult and things get edges and contracts are binding and your identity gets tighter as your history cannibalizes your future and there's less room to stretch out and breathe deep—but of course, that is only looking at it one way.

In another way, there are depths in the tightness and passion in the exactitude, and an adult can still be a child whenever he wants; the only difference is that now he has become his own parent, and his adult self cares for the safety and hunger of his child self.

He is grown up
and powerful
to play his role
in society,
but still young
and curious
to step into a forest
on the weekend
and hug a tree
as if it were all
for the first time.

Time.

I work up my temporal strength
to hold on to a moment;
I revel in the feeling of pain
or meditate in the heights
or even listen to silence
to slow the clock hands.

But as soon as I get hold of one moment,
the next few pass quickly.
And they always pass eventually,
even the ones that pass slow.

So inevitably it seems
time has gone by
all at once.

Life.

A day is a microcosm for a life,
an hour for a day,
and so on.

Before breakfast,
I've got a body full of energy
and a day to be created.

At lunch,
ends my young morning life
and begins my afternoon age.

After dinner,
closing my eyes
to rejoin the rest.

I wake again and again;
I live again and again.

Once more,
an awed child in the morning,
a hungry youngster before lunch,
an old man in the afternoon,
an elderly soul in the night.

Night.

In the night,
breathing slow,
content anytime
to close my eyes
and sleep.

I find all of history in a moment.
I've already lived so many lives,
and died every night.

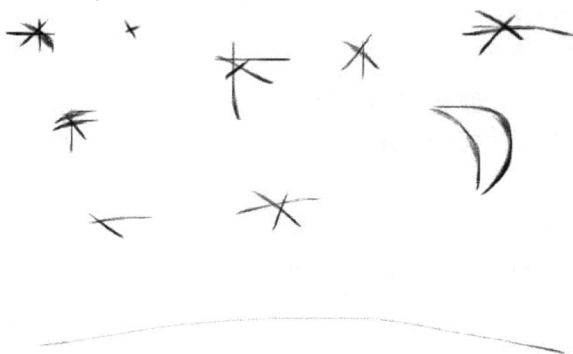

Nostalgia.

I long for classics
and get nostalgic
when I remember:
what is now
will be a past
in the future.

Backwards,
without a forward opposite:
longing for what is still to come,
as for what already has.

Like a thought you can't remember:
it's there, but not really;
it's yours, but it's not.

So far close:
to see, not taste;
remember, not live.

Like her hair and his smile,
the wet smell of cider, the sound of warmth,
and all else that made the day what it was.

All else, except that it was;
and the memory you're left with
isn't the real thing.

This.

This,
has never happened before
and will never happen again.

Or,
it always has
and always will.

Fleeting.

Fight the fleetingness,
but what persists?

The most principled man;
his habits fade.

And the strongest,
eventually weakens.

And the wisest,
eventually forgets.

Travel.

I am keen to be going
somewhere: traveling, spatially.
For even when
I rest: I travel. in time.

This timely going forward, I enjoy less,
but am glad for the motivation
to get up, and travel again.

In a new time and place,
I feel as if I'm living
for the first time.

Everything is loud and bright,
as if I'm really just starting
to listen and see
for the first time.

Like your newborn self
saw the world:
without all the experience
of the world as it is;
without so many memories
to assure you
that this is
the way
things are.

Travel cont.

To both see things anew,
and for what we know them as:
we usually only do the latter,
but have to sacrifice it
when we choose to do the former.

I notice the leaves anew. Green is not just green, but that which fills the shapes of what I have since called leaves. I am seeing them again for the first time. And the whole world seems sublime all of a sudden. So much that I forget what it means when the light turns green at the traffic stop and I am not sure whether to stop or go.

But still, in a new time and place, how quickly things become old and routine—so that your mind need only travel familiar pathways. As time goes on, I notice fewer particulars, and melt slowly into a general feeling. It is subtle and alluring until I am not aware of time passing at all, and then something shocks me and wakes me up to my subconscious routine and I know I must travel again.

When I return, I say a prayer: God, please don't let me lose this newness of vision. Please let me see the world like the first time, like I'm traveling to a place I've never been before, when the world fills up with possibilities and I see more paths than the routine one. God, please don't let me lose this newness of vision.

Homesickness.

I am less homesick nowadays. Everything seems to be more of the same. More easily I sleep in a new place: in the grass by the fountain at the little French town across the bay.

Less anxious to travel far away, more understanding of people different from myself and places other than where I grew up. More comfortable in each of many places, more a dweller of the earth than just of my hometown.

I imagine I might be homesick to leave earth, to travel in space or visit another planet. But now I have learned to stretch myself and adapt. Even far away from earth I would only be homesick for a little while until I made alien friends and learned to walk with less gravity and breathe with less oxygen.

Nature.

On the out-hike,
our boots on a forward tilt
crushing wet redwood.

Early in the morning,
to reach the shore
before sundown
we keep a quick pace.

She says,
between deep breaths,
"I'm not feeling anything
but my biology."

A pine branch
waves its needle fingers.
A brown leaf
kicks up in the wind.

On the shore,
we stand inside
a stump's stomach.

She points,
at cloud tails
that moustache
the mountain faces.

Nature cont.

Even amid tall trees
and wide rivers,
I look at my feet.

Retreat into myself,
a perceiving thing,
and a thing to be perceived,
without sense of which is which
—other than some vague memory
of an upright man
that emerged wiser
from the woods.

Breath.

Cross-legged, sitting up straight, moving my belly: out to inhale and in to exhale. Even saying silently those two words—"in" and "out"—so that my nomenclatured mind has something to hold.

The inhale is long and the exhale is slow. A breathing more floating, less swimming; drifting, without any speed or particular direction.

My nostrils, like the gears of a pulley system, lift a plane of awareness from where my legs press against the shore to the tallest hair on my head.

At first the inhale is a sort of "pulling" or "sucking" of air into the nostrils, while the exhale is a sort of "pushing" or "blowing."

Then changes the "pushing" exhale into a "sighing"—the same muscle contraction that you use to breathe out of your mouth only that your mouth is closed so the air flows out of your nose.

The "pushing" is deeper—more from your belly and back of your throat than in the nostrils. And the air swirls about in your head as a more open cavity before "flowing" out of your nostrils—this, instead of a "rushing" out as with the previous "pushing" exhale.

Breath cont.

And changes the "pulling" inhale into an "opening"—like water dammed up, the air is all around the body ready to come in, and the inhale opens the dam. Less of a mechanical force and more like magnetism in the bottom of your belly which attracts the air.

A softer, slower and longer breathing, moving in and out of your lungs at the same pace it moves in the open air.

An opening and allowing in, and a sighing and allowing out. This kind of breath has less noise and movement, less to hear and feel.

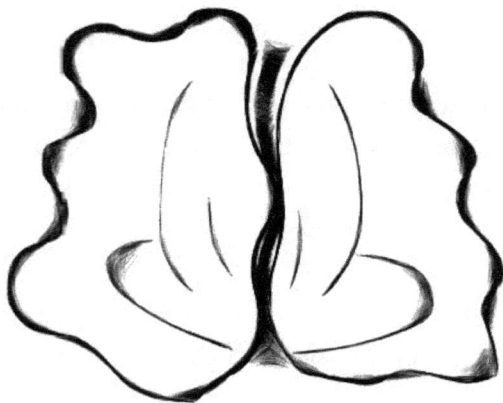

Meditation.

Removing one sense at a time: in a quiet place, with nothing in my mouth, hearing and tasting have gone; smelling, even though the air is pine-scented, has lost my attention.

I am left with the feel of my breath and the sight of my eyelids—standing on two sensory legs.

The breath, to my surprise, goes before the sight, falling vaguely down below—so that I am now standing on one leg in tree pose, figuratively; still sitting cross-legged, actually.

With only one sense left, I know that after this is the void. An intense focus on one thing precedes the same focus on nothing. I rest and balance, then slowly, bend my knee, and jump ... up and out of my senses.

It is like "arriving" at a plateau. Your consciousness explodes out of the center of your forehead and it becomes like a dream of nothing, insofar as you still certainly "are" and seem to be experiencing, but don't know what—without your senses.

Thinking.

For some time, I don't know how long, or where. Until, with even my autonomous energies lifted up and out of "myself," I realize I've forgotten to breathe.

And with the "realized," before I can stop it, I clutch for my senses and start to "think" about what might happen if I hold my breath.

And with the first thought come many more, like the space inside my skull is so used to having such a mass that when all of a sudden it is gone there is leftover gravity that opens a big black hole, making it impossible to stop the mental passersby.

Memory.

My memory cuts through the shallow recent into the deeper past. When I deny my mind its easy present bias, still it wants something to hold, and is not satisfied with just a simple focus on the breath.

So, it reaches deeper and wider, dodging the defenses that protect my meditation and pulling memories from my childhood which I didn't even know I still had, memories which are much more poignant and effective at breaking my concentration and occupying my thought.

Consciousness.

You look out at the space in front of your eyes and wonder if it's real and three-dimensional, or if it's all just a two-dimensional painting right on top of your eyeballs, or if your eyeballs and the rest of your body are just a projection of your brain, or if your brain itself is a projection—so that it's all the manifestation of a Consciousness that's really not physical at all.

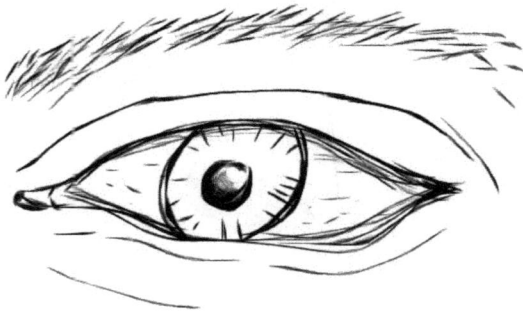

Part II: Noon

Writing.

Sitting facing out the street front window in a coffee shop in Chicago, the guy at the counter behind me talks to the barista. I am at once *hearing* him speak through my ears and simultaneously *seeing* the words type out, even the quotation marks.

I assign a verb to *how* he said it—he "whispered" to the barista. Though it was not, in this reality, so sensual an encounter. If I were trying to write the reality, I would have written: he "talked with a patronizing tone" to the barista.

I write this down
on a little piece of paper
behind my eyelids
and fold it back
to remember.

To write,
I go to the symphony,
watch a beggar beg,
close my eyes,
listen to my breath,
watch myself, watching
everything else.

Writing cont.

"Pinched"
—in between
uncomfortable to be inspired
and comfortable to be physically able to write.

I touch it lightly,
only when I'm feeling good
—so as not to stain it,
when I'm feeling bad.

I get up and out of it,
focus on something else
live another life;
then return like a tourist
and find it anew
—to read
a different writer.

Up and out of it all,
to grab onto something original
and then endure a great anxiety
to pull it back down
and spread it out.

Words.

I like to let every word do its heavy lifting all alone. There are certain common words that have so much meaning, so that when you toss them in with each other they cannibalize their neighbors.

One word all alone on a blank page, like one barracuda in a big fish tank; you don't even think: what happened to all the other fish?

Our barracudas aren't the same. "Love" seems to be a universal barracuda; "death" too. And any other word that is only several letters but is so fat and swollen with meaning—not because of its objective musicality or calligraphy. But because of its subjective human value— the meaning and memories from a lifetime called forth when the lifeform thinks, reads, sings, or says it.

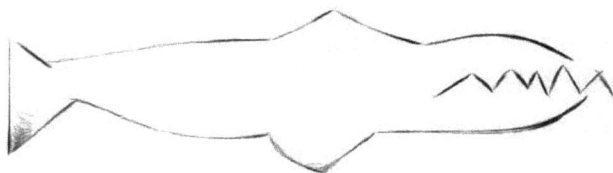

Nonsense.

Each own its on, word, meaning has—so that a sentence all out of order which most people would say doesn't make sense, still does.

Not total gibberish: still words, spaces, and punctuation; still puzzle pieces, just not put together "right."

Like a Picasso woman with her face all jumbled up—not a total indiscernible mess: still colors and borders and distinguishable parts. Just not exactly where the parts "belong," i.e., where we're used to seeing them.

Samely, each letter has a meaning, especially its sound. So that I could create a dwor that does not exist in the English language, and you would say that is not a dwor. But already you are associating it with dwors that sound like it and have letters in common.

And further, when I start to use the new dwor consistently in the same contexts then you would build up a memory of the dwor and understand the situations in which I was using it and open up unusual corners of our language which represent parts of your mind that you didn't know and even say for yourself, "That is not a dwor!"

Names.

We like to be able to call it something; necessary, to categorize the world and learn. Even though, as Sartre says, things are divorced from their names—form doesn't match function; the physical thing isn't represented in the sound (except maybe in the case of onomatopoeias).

Further, we often use the name of a Form to describe a particular thing. For example, a "tree" is not just a "tree." It may be an "oak." But still more—a six-year-old, twenty-foot-tall *Quercus stellata*. And still more, until eventually it escapes description.

And further still, the names are human-centric. A plant is "green" because that's the way human eyes take in its light on the frequency spectrum. A plant is "food" because we need to eat. But is a plant either of these objectively and apart from us?

There seems to be a hierarchy of meaning from names: highest, there is the kind where we do not name it at all—this is what Nietzsche recommends for naming virtues. In the middle, is a diversity of names that allows for some differentiation—this we do with books and people. We say this book is nonfiction and its subject is automobiles; that person is a mechanic and a deist.

Names cont.

We say as if this nomenclature is exhaustively and perfectly descriptive; though it comes closer than the lowest, it is not perfect. And the lowest, when we have one name for a diverse thing.

In English, we have one name for love, as if it were describing one thing. We bring our "love" to the herd as if we had it in common with them. We say, "I am in love!" As if it means the same thing. And we set parameters, guidelines and expectations that are the averages of other loves—most usually those loves nearest to our time and place.

So too with justice. When someone says, "That is just!" The most appropriate response is: "What exactly do you mean by justice?"

Just as I am, and you are, and your identity is, something like a Form with many different renderings in reality—so that your name is convenient and practical, but not necessarily true, depending on what you mean by calling yourself by it.

Art.

Like all the memory and meaning of life
contrasted by the chaos and confusion of death,
all the science of the real world
just so slightly undone in a piece of art.

Is "art" not necessarily a human thing end-to-end? A
word we created to describe things that are, only because
we perceive them to be, if *esse est percipi*.

Human art is pseudo creation. I, as a writer, did not
invent language. And you, as a painter, did not invent
color.

The humanist will say, look, we invented these words and
assigned sounds to things; language is ours. And look, we
made these paints and designed shapes; color is ours.

But no human is responsible for the material world nor
for his own ability to mold and craft it. We do not create
so much as we rearrange what has already been created.
And even the agency for such rearranging may be outside
ourselves.

So that the true artist instructs her students: let it flow
through you, rather than try and grasp and wield all of it
at once, all by yourself; splash delicately on the surface,
making new ripples in an age-old ocean.

Artist.

The artist tells me that she has to travel to another world anytime she creates, and it makes her sick, like homesickness. When she travels to that other world of genuine creation, she misses the world of custom, conditioning, past history and proven correlation in which we are accustomed to living.

So quickly she rings up a man to have in her bed to feel his real body, or meets her real friends to have real conversation about real things, or to grab handfuls of the real grass and smell the real trees—letting her real body experience the real world that someone else created, vacationing from playing god herself. But this is only the halfway solution for an artist, she tells me.

The greatest pleasure is the combination of the two worlds: instead of fleeing her created world to return to the real world, the inhabitants of the real world come to her created world to live in it for a while and it becomes real for them.

This is when she really transcends: from a halfway human to a full world creator. And she delights in her own reality substantiated by those who come to live in it. But of course, her visitors have their own travels and cannot stay. And she cannot live in her own world alone.

I.

I am,
after all,
still human,
she says,
and prefer
to live in His,
just as much as they
prefer to live in mine.

Sculptor.

The sculptor says to the artist, I see. Your paintings are much like my statues.

He explains to her how it was necessary that he became like them before he could sculpt the world.

A sculptor can only create the object with a great amount of time alone. But the object always has a subject.

And he cannot possibly know what it looks and feels like without subjecting himself to the subject which he must remember when creating the object alone.

He gets down and in to live it, learns it in a language that can be understood, then goes away to render it in his art form. When finished, he must come back again to get more. He must be alone and away from it all to create, but only after being deeply with and part of everything.

Morality.

A moralist Father and his Son walk along the lakefront.

Son holds a rock.

Father looks nervously at the rock in Son's hand, "Son, do not throw that rock."

At once, Son shifts the rock from his left to his dominant right, skips toward the water and throws the rock impressively far into the center of the lake.

Father is shocked, then angry, "Son! I just told you that you cannot."

Son, smiling even wider at the game, says, "But of course I can, Father." He points out to the center of the lake, "Just look at the ripples in the water from where it splashed."

Realizing he had misspoken, Father struggles to explain, "What I meant to say, Son, was that you *should* not."

Son, confused, asks, "But what does that mean, Father?"

Father thinks—of his own upbringing and schooling, of his experiences and identity; why he did the things he had, who told him to, and how he got to where he was.

Morality cont.

Still, Son looks up, waiting for an answer.

Father breathes deeply, and says only this, "What I meant to say, Son, is that *I would prefer* if you didn't throw rocks."

At once, Son smiles and jumps into Father's arms, "Oh Father, well then of course I won't!"

Choices.

This time, place, mind, and body chose me. Still, I have choices: yes or no, left or right. But how? Other than according to those things which already chose me.

So, I wonder: is my attempt to resist conditioning, itself conditioned? If I can't wiggle a random variable outside the causal chain: past, experiencing present, and becoming future.

My past created
by other pasts,
borrowed atoms,
and taught thoughts.

When I ask myself, "What should I do?" My next question is: which one of me is the "I" referring to? And then: from which morality is the "should" derived?

Everything is a choice. Sitting still is a choice. Not choosing is a choice. It is the nature of a spatial thing that, in time, it is always choosing—every moment affecting what is: ourselves and everything else.

Still, I wonder: who (or what) is doing the choosing? Ourselves, something else, or nothing at all?

Fork.

Two roads diverge:
I try not to worry
about choosing a road
and instead focus
on the fork itself,
so that I find myself
all of a sudden
at another fork
and so start
to focus on this fork
just the same as the last.

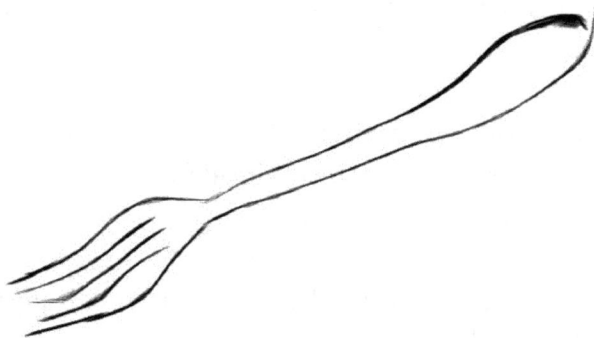

Boyhood.

For a while,
when I was just
a physical young boy
—this was before
I met my mental
—I was happy
just to run around
and chase my instincts.

But as I learned, sometimes a thought overwhelmed my instinct. The only trouble was that there were so many thoughts, and contradictions among them.

The mere fact there were so many wouldn't have been any trouble on its own; it was the contradictions that really hurt.

And by that point, I had learned enough to believe that truth was important. But I had already started to doubt the "truths" I had from before.

And so began a very painful skepticism which anyone must undergo who has learned certain cultural norms and traditions without proof. Only thereafter, could I return to the same sureness of my boyhood.

Martyr.

A Christian martyr who disobeys a king who threatens him with death if he does not adopt the state religion, and an atheist who disobeys a God who gives him an ultimatum—what is the difference between the two?

Is not an atheist a saint by the same definition? Choosing the long death of hell, in exchange for a humanist life on earth.

I wonder:
in a long hell,
is suffering still suffering?
Without any contrasting pleasure.

And if the cause of hell is to fall into certain vices on earth, assuming these "vices" are actually some of the fruits of human life.

Might we claim our heaven now?
And suffer eternally.

Absurdism.

Instinct is the moral code born in us; survival is its supreme value. As society became essential for survival, a new moral code of social law sometimes superseded instinct.

More recently, social tradition has been superseded by reason; its supreme value is truth—but a certain absurdism comes from there being nothing certainly true about reason applied to human behavior, i.e., morality.

There are laws for a healthy human life; and there is truth. And they are not always the same—is this the absurdist claim?

There is a way to be, even in the modern world, to satisfy our age-old instincts; and then there are higher values up and out of and, sometimes, directly counter to our base, yet healthy, animality.

Health.

A new friend tells me that she just wants to have the highest quality of life possible, and she uses her biological remnants as her guide.

She *feels* like there is a right way to live but doesn't *think* so. She says, it's difficult to live, however, without a sense that there is—a right way.

Chesterton would say to her, "In these cases it is not enough that the unhappy man should desire truth; he must desire health. Nothing can save him but a blind hunger for normality, like that of a beast."

Some cases of mental "illness" are such that, in regard to some part of his conditioning, the invalid has forgotten how to be human. Thus, the illness is only relative to a certain "normal" humanity.

I myself am lucky that my soul is subjected to needs that my body can satisfy ... but then I wonder if my body just satisfies the needs that it can, and these are those which my soul accepts as its own.

Hunger.

I think of hunger
and feel my palette
chase down to my teeth.

Higher, however,
I have less and less
hunger for the taste.

I know I'm no longer thirsty
when I've forgotten my cup
and picked it up by accident
to find there is still some drink left.

Feeling and thinking
for emotions and ideas,
while our instincts
are just trying
to survive.

Dogma.

"Everything we take as dogma is only custom … Everything we take as dogma is only custom," and he kept repeating this, with his eyes closed, focusing on his breath.

When he opened his eyes, they were looking at his folded hands, which no longer made sense. They were creepy crawly things, really only one peachy blob when folded together like this.

Surely, this was not the way. At least not for he as alive and man, not dead or God. Surely, there is dogma. He closed his eyes again: "There is dogma … There is dogma … And it is true."

When he opened his eyes again, his hands each had five fingers again, and he remembered their uses: a thumb pacifier for his younger self and an index he used for pointing in school—such ideas that only make sense in a world with dogma.

Existentialism.

Sartre says, man first exists, encounters himself, then surges up. But he leaves out intermediaries. First man exists, yes—but in what sense? Then, not yet himself, man encounters the others; necessary, he would die very young without them.

The true test, then, is a secondary non-existence, to walk into the woods, physically a grown man, but nothing in any other sense, and say to Her, "Mother Earth, am I you, or am I?" Only thereafter can he surge up and define himself

Identity.

On the 13th floor of the library there are four corners, each with a desk that faces a window. I set my bag and coat in the southeast corner and leave them there to walk the shelves. I pick up a few books, read two or three lines, and put them back. I wander in and out of the bookshelves until I'm lost.

I gather my bearings and walk toward what I believe to be the southeast corner, only to find someone already sitting there. My first conclusion is not that I have by accident come upon the northwest corner, but that I, my physical self, had never actually left the southeast corner, and now I, the wandering soul, am happening upon myself from the outside.

But as I approach, I realize this man's body is heavier than mine and he wears glasses. So I say, that is not I.

I, who, instead of maintaining a thin frame and good eyesight, had gained weight and come to need glasses, consider that it very well could be.

And so I think for a moment that my wandering soul might inhabit this body just the same as it might find the true southeast corner and re-inhabit the other.

Change.

There are those things that you wish to know and experience, but in doing so, you can never be the same.

It's the paradox of learning in reverse: it might be bad or good, but how can you know until you've done it?

And once you've found out,
it's already happened;
so that now you've gotten
up and outside
and seen the trick,
and it is only by great effort
that you may get
back down and in
to fool yourself again.

Potential.

With one or a few certainties,
ignorant, consciously or not,
I do not know in most cases,
of the many other potentialities,
which, together with their certainties,
comprise the whole.

Potentialities,
are certainties,
with all the same parts
except for reality;
and is not reality
so dubious a thing
that we might say
potentialities
are, in fact,
certainties?

Such that,
certain people
live sixteenths of lives,
or much smaller fractions,
without filling up
with all the rest,
other than their own
history and conditioning.

Fashion.

Of all the collisions
of condition and environment,
he chooses the fashionable one
to please his time and place.

That he has one history
is not the warrant for this,
for his one history
is filled with multitudes.

Only alone,
does he think
that I have a style;
that I have a sound,
genes and history
—bothers me a little,
to be so tied down.

Mirror.

She wasn't so much herself as she was a mirror that remembered. It's just that she would rather experience someone else, and so built herself up to attract others: beautiful to see beauty; intelligent to hear intelligence.

But when it came time to decide what to show back to them, she was only ever a chameleon, or a mirror that talked like a parrot.

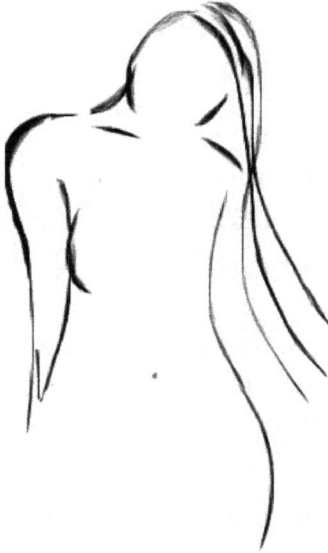

Spatiotemporal.

I've met a hundred men
who've said they could do it,
if in an instant;
only they forget:
it is the time and space
which is ours;
so to say
such and such
if only in a moment,
or in a molecule
—is not heroic,
not even human;
is a non-phrase.

If given a choice between: all the pain for the rest of my
life played out moderately over time, or experienced
excruciatingly all at once; I'd take it all at once.

But only because I know my capacities for experience in
any one moment are limited—such that, while certainly
the worst pain I'd ever experience, it would only be
marginally worse than my second worst pain, and
thereafter would be all over so I'd never feel pain again.

By the same logic, I'd take my pleasures just the opposite:
played out over time.

Spatiotemporal cont.

Even the worst pain,
so quickly,
is not so bad;
just the same as
pleasure is better
over time.

It is the time,
the extended
playing out,
the endurance
—that makes it human.

The language itself,
the human experience
—is spatiotemporal.

Wide.

He asks, how would you like it?
I say, I would like it to be wide,
if we can manage.

Well, of course,
we can manage,
says the old man,
but I wonder,
do you have enough
with which to fill it?

Oh, don't worry about that, I say,
a thing like this will fill itself.

The old man sighs and says,
as he would to his own child,
don't make the same mistake that I did.

While you are young
you must stay close
to your own "I."

It is the slice of god
closest to your own
eyes and ears.

Part III: Evening

Writer.

I am, at any one time, "acting" as one of my characters. I am always "the Writer," the prime mover of my portfolio of selves, the initial cause of behavioral effects.

All that remains is whether I myself am "the Writer." Or if He is, or you are, or maybe we share the same One.

If one student was the whole, a studier of everything; across time, a renaissance man, with all these studies within him, but at once more like a Chameleon, able to blend in with any field.

Limited, only spatiotemporally, from being everyone— who is, has been and could be—at once, in one body and mind.

Chameleon.

The Chameleon who changes his color with his surroundings—what color is the Chameleon if there were no colors? Would the Chameleon cease to exist, take on the color of nothingness, or remember his past colors and choose one to wear?

Does the Chameleon not grow large as a dragon, swelling with all of his environment? Or does he merely contain the facade of each identity within him?

Or actually becomes the green frog, the yellow canary, the blue bluebird. Or is he always merely the Chameleon, not an actual shape-shifter, but only a master of disguise changing his mask?

If the Writer
is indeed the One,
and the Chameleon
is just the spatiotemporal slice
of the One
at any given time and space.

Is the Writer the Chameleon,
with only guises over time?
Or is he God,
with all of it at once?

Here, I'd like to include a note from a friend on how she understands the Chameleon:

So much of how we understand the nature of the Chameleon depends on the boundaries that we perceive to be significant—for example, we perceive a clear boundary between the colors green and yellow, or even the emotions of empathy and frustration.

However, it is interesting to consider that these boundaries are artificial in a sense—although we may perceive some sort of difference/shift, that perception itself is a function of our ability to exist in a world of entropy where categories, names, and boundaries help us make sense of things.

Is it beneficial that we take these boundaries and categories for granted? Is it useful to accept them to relate to others? Alternatively, is it more beneficial to challenge our very understanding that we may be acting like Chameleons, as we may perhaps be quite consistently expressing a sentiment or idea of the same origin that manifests in quite different ways in different spatiotemporal moments?

Trust.

She asks, is this a mask?
He says no.
She asks, might it be a mask
that is telling me it is not?
He says yes.

Whereas I might show myself to be deeply intimate and successfully empathic with another's experience, but at once as I remove that mask and put on another, my partner, seeing me switch guises so smoothly, might ask how many guises there are.

She believes not that I still wear the face she loves under my secondary mask, but that there are a third, fourth, and many more.

Face.

Do you believe
there is some core
to our being?

A face
under a finite
number of masks.

One big soul,
for all men;
all faces,
the same man.

Friends.

I met a man who said, "I am A."

And I replied, "Ah, my friend! I am also A."

And he exclaimed, "It is always nice to meet another A!"

And we talked and talked and slapped each other's shoulders. Until along came another man.

He said to us, "I am B."

And I replied to the newcomer, "Ah, my friend! I am also B."

And the newcomer exclaimed, "It is wonderful to meet another B!"

But now the old A looked at me with scorn and questioned, "I thought you were A?"

And I replied, "My friend, I am both."

And now both A and B looked with scorn and left me.

We.

His lover asks, "Who are you really?"

At first, he starts to explain pedantically based on psychology and philosophy. But she says, "No, that is your scholarly and learned self."

And then he laughs and touches her arm affectionately. But she says, "No, that is your sexual self."

And then like an animal trying to escape he becomes each one: the artist, the thinker, the child, the husband, the businessman, the politician, the lover—and gives an explanation for each.

But she says again, "No, who are you really?"

And still he tries more, and as he does his pupils widen and she sees through them and inside into what looks like an old-fashioned shutter camera that clicks and clicks and reveals each of him.

Until finally his pupils start to dilate and almost none of the color of his eyes is left and the camera shutters one last time and what comes next is not another photo of an identity but just a bright light.

We cont.

And the brightness shines from his eyes onto her face and she says, "Oh, there you are."

And feels not that she is looking at him any longer but that they are together in the brightness—two, and many more, becoming One.

And that is when she really understands and says, "Oh, there We are."

You.

When I am here with you,
especially one person,
even more so my love,
I am here with you fully.

When I am not with you,
even when I sit with you physically,
I am somewhere else entirely.

Our.

If we are to say our love, is the "our" not just you and I? Or do we include the rest of them? Surely not; else, I'd be dishonest to say, I love you.

I might instead say, I love "them." Or, if I don't know myself either, I might say, they love them.

But still we seem to say only two: you and I: ours. Then why do we use their ideas about it; what do they know?

Only when we are enough ourselves, may we call it ours, and so really have two, that become One.

Feel.

The verb "feel" has two meanings. In one way, it describes one of the five senses—the sensation of touch—alongside the other sensory verbs: see, hear, taste, and smell.

In another, it is emotion—which has everything, and nothing, to do with the five senses, touch especially.

I tell her this,
and she responds:
feel as emotion
is the senses
interacting within
your heart.

So I ask:
but what's the causality
between senses and heart?

She asks:
is "causality"
the right word?

Love.

It begins
with a building up
of potential and power.

Flowing up
from the earth
through the soles
of your feet.

From another soul
through their eyes
and into yours.

Learning to hold potential realities,
your mind fills with experience:
your whole being swells
with the reality
that flows in
through the senses.

It grows within you
and wants to get out
and return to the rest,
but you must hold it,
letting it stretch you.

Love cont.

The reality you hold
enters its own home;
you carry Her
like a welcome guest.

It grows
and pours in
through your eyes,
ears, and skin.

Together with reality,
taking mutual pleasure
that it is held within you
but also at the same time
within Her.

Together,
breaking down
physical laws
that two
cannot be one

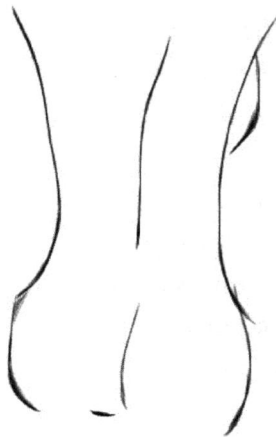

Empathy.

I love that when you meet someone new and you really meet them, they become the most interesting person in the world for a few minutes.

And if you really listen you fall into their pupils opened wide like windows and take up residence in their home and look back out through the peephole at yourself rapping on the front door asking to be let in.

At first,
their pupils
like black glass
reflective like a mirror,
you will see yourself;
then look deeper,
their pupils
like dark pools
that open up;
swim through.

Her.

"What on earth are you doing out here in the cold without your coat?"

Shivering, cupping her coffee, she looks up out of a trance and smiles.

"I'm writing," she says simply, as if I should have known.

"What," I begin to stutter an objection.

She smiles at my misunderstanding and raises her index finger to tap on her temple.

"Oh," I whisper.

I was in a holy place.

So I took off my coat and sat next to her.

Society.

The crowd walked
in a tunnel with an echo
and at first everyone chanted
the same chant that one person had started
but then more individuals got creative
and started a diversity of chants
and the competing songs
created a dissonance
that killed the chants
altogether.

Alone.

Like Camus' townspeople of Oran,
plague-ridden and isolated:
"It dawned on him that
he and the man with him
weren't talking about the same thing
… and the attempt to communicate
had to be given up."

First, our perception is different:
you and I, see the same painting
two different ways.

Second, our description is different:
even if we used the same words,
they wouldn't mean the same thing.

So that,
to communicate
a painter
must make
two translations,
both impossible:
first, from her own mind
to the canvas;
second, from the canvas
to the viewer's mind.

Psychosis.

Psychosis is unhealthy in solitude for the psychotic is out of touch with the physical reality where his physical body exists.

Psychosis is unhealthy in society for the psychotic is illiterate in the reality that others seem to have agreed upon.

If there is objective reality, we are all psychotic, because our subjective worlds as they appear to us are not necessarily the worlds that are.

Assuming then, that the average of our many subjectivities trends towards objectivity, each of us cures our unique psychosis by empathy.

We come closer to reality through understanding and conversing with others. So that even if there is no objective reality, at least we are together, and have agreed on the same delusion.

Part IV: Man

Apartment.

I used to have a plant
that sat on my bookshelf.

I believed,
whether it is true or not,
that it made me healthier:
to have some nature,
inside my apartment.

Only that,
some mornings
when I left for work,
I'd forget to open the blinds
for my plant to get light.

And some nights
when I'd get home,
I'd be so tired
that I'd forget
to give it water.

So that, the plant
may have been healthy for me,
inside my apartment;
but my apartment,
was not healthy for the plant.

Apartment cont.

One day, I opened the glass door to my balcony, and set the plant outside, to get sun all day and water from the rain. I planned to bring it back inside the next morning, but have now left it outside on the balcony for several weeks. I can still see it out there through the glass door.

Shower.

In the shower,
with peppermint
soap stinging
and smelling
like sharp air.

In the shower,
in the bathroom,
in my apartment,
on the floor,
twenty-two floors
above the ground
—what delivered us here?

So high above the ground.

Handstand.

On Friday,
in my apartment
I stand on my hands
and let the blood rush
from my heart
to my head.

Coming of age
in modern America:
I met a man
who said,
he was not
so much one
as he was three.

The animal
who needs to eat,
the working man
who does his job,
and the creative god
who stretches his arms
on the weekends.

Weekend.

On Saturday,
my exhaustion catches up to me,
so that after I've made my breakfast,
before I've had my coffee,
when I've read a few pages,
I'll lay down to rest,
and not wake up
until it's dark.

On Sunday,
after a lethargic Saturday
I wake up and fight to return;
sitting up straight
in the early morning,
enduring to do my work,
—for two hours, uncomfortable
and not enjoying myself.

Then all of a sudden,
the whole world returns
so that I can write again,
and the blurry edges
are sharp again
at 9:45 a.m.

Pinched.

I'm usually very clean and fed
and safe and satisfied.

Living in the city
this weird romantic lifestyle
where I'm so well cared for
that I float away from
my body and its needs.

Comfortably within the system
carried along by my genes and upbringing
and everything that's already been done.

I don't mind keeping a job
just so I stay "tethered" and "pinched"
in a world of angles and boundaries and numbers.

In the crowd at a show
the speakers so loud that I can't hear
I fall asleep and let the crowd hold me up.

I wake up in my bed on Monday morning,
put on a shirt, and call a car to the office.

Jackhammer.

A giant industrial jackhammer
machine guns down
a highway bridge
that no longer fits
in the city's plans.

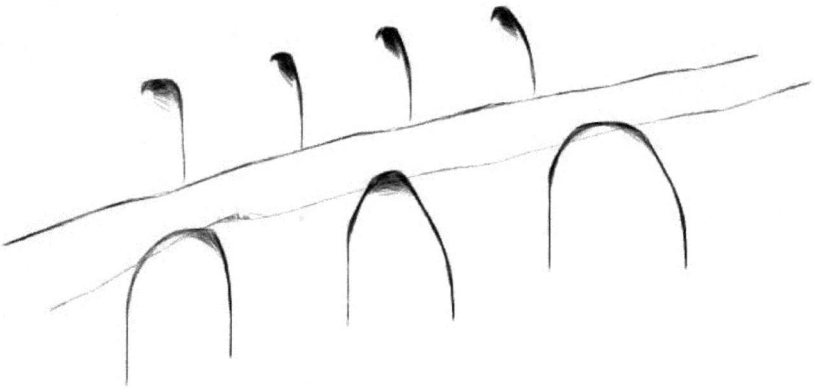

Cog.

A cog,
on the correct gear,
in the correct machine,
in the correct factory.

In the queue,
thankful for comrades,
ahead and behind.

In his place,
waiting,
for something,
he doesn't know
what for;
so he works,
in the meantime.

Starve.

Artists starve
more often
than bankers;
even though,
the less successful bankers
don't buy art,
and the more successful artists
don't starve.

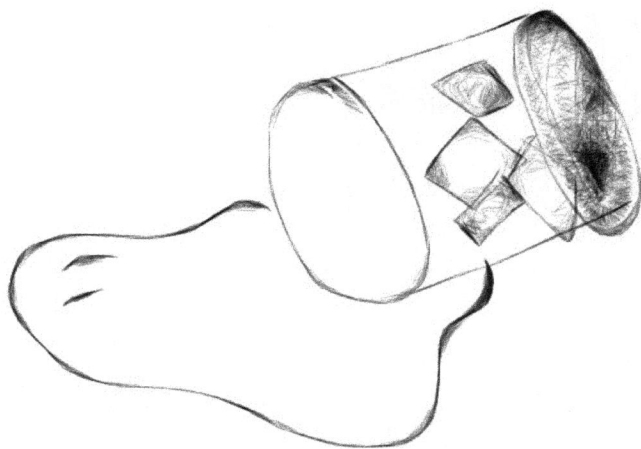

Three.

Animal bodies
and god souls,
with human minds
stretched in between.

On the survival paradigm:
good, being satiation;
and bad, lack thereof
—this is morality
relative to our animal natures
just trying to survive.

On the first physical plane,
I pursue the "good"
for which I am conditioned.

On the second mental plane,
I pursue also the "bad"
because it amplifies the "good."

On the third spiritual plane,
I begin to rise up
and out of "good" and "bad"
and into wonder and awe and gratitude.

Three cont.

On the first plane,
I take hot showers.

On the second plane,
I take cold showers
to amplify my hot showers.

And on the third plane,
the shower is neither hot nor cold
but only water, for which I am thankful.

Sleep.

I think about dying
when I'm really sleepy;
I think maybe it wouldn't be so bad.

Like I am happy to sleep,
when I've been awake too long.

I am not satisfied
nor do I seek satisfaction;
I am depleted.
ready for the dark and quiet
for a little while.

Duality.

Living and dying:
are the ground standing up
and the sky falling down.

Living and dying are the same thing;
sometimes one shows its face more than the other,
sometimes you feel light and sometimes you feel heavy.

Life is a long day,
and death is a longer night.

Survival.

To survive,
is to keep
two worlds
—body and soul
—together.

Soul reaches down
through the mind
and grabs hold of the body.

When someone dies
their soul lets go.

Suicide.

She wanted to kill herself,
and so we argued:
I for life,
and her for
whatever is after.

She killed herself,
and left me this note:
"If only you could've
argued better for life."

Earthquake.

I died in an earthquake tonight. My older self, up in my childhood bathroom shaving. When the house at 267 N. Sumac started to shake.

At first not serious—or at least seeming not to be, so that I even considered finishing my shave, to avoid leaving the bathroom and going downstairs with shaving cream still on my neck.

But then I stepped out of the bathroom to look out the window that faced the driveway and saw large cracks forming quickly all up and down the cul-de-sac.

I left the shaving cream on my neck and went quickly down the stairs—*quickly*, like in a dream, or a film, when characters go quickly, but the watchers watch slowly.

In my mind played a safety video of what to do in an earthquake and it said to get low to the ground and underneath a solid structure and whatever you do don't fall in the cracks.

By then, I was at the main floor, in the waiting room at the bottom of the stairs and in between the front door, dining room and living room, my house was filled with everyone I had ever known running every which way.

Earthquake cont.

At this point the house was still all together, and I was thinking to get as low to the ground as possible, so I started down the stairs to the basement.

It was then that everything opened up, and the section of the basement stairs where I was standing broke off and I started to fall.

The whole fall before I woke up lasted about fifteen seconds and these were my thoughts as my death seemed to be as real as I imagine it will actually be someday:

In the first five seconds, I had two thoughts: feeling myself to be like the character who dies first in a film, I thought how had I forgotten the very simple instruction from the safety video—don't fall in the cracks!

But then I started to quickly replay the event and realized that such a big section of the basement stairs had broken off in a place that was no less reasonable for me to be than any other at that exact moment, and so then I started to think: why me?

In the next five seconds: I heard from above my classmate Ashley shout down, as if she was leaning at the edge of the crack, risking her life to shout down to me in a very short, calm and somber tone.

Earthquake cont.

Not shrill or terrified as you would expect—she shouted down, "Goodbye, Cole." And I started to think of all the people that I would miss.

In the last five seconds: I started to think that I was really dying. I had fallen very far by this time and everything was red and hot but still I grabbed for the rocky edges of the earth's insides to stop my fall.

But then looked up and realized I had fallen too far and was going too fast and even if I did stop myself would not be able to make the climb back up.

This is when I felt what I imagine it will actually feel like to die someday, after all the hysteria of the first ten seconds passes and I've tried to avoid it and thought about what could have gone differently and start to feel sorry for myself, then I will really start to face it and be overwhelmed by a sadness and sense of loss that is too much for a human and so is really the final blow—that sadness itself, which tears soul from body.

And even now as I write this at 4:19 a.m. in my safe, blue, cool bed I am starting to think already of the coming workday and so forgetting such a valuable lesson of the red and hot dying.

Earthquake cont.

I write this to contain the sense of gratitude I feel for the life I have left to live.

Now waking after what was a 15-second death as real as I imagine the real one will be someday.

Only that I have already forgotten—not completely but enough so that the big and sharp mountain that it was has been carved and sanded down into one of many small mnemonic pebbles.

And naturally so, as such a sense of gratitude which I tried to contain is the complement of the sense of loss which bore it—such a sense seems to me now as the largest emotion possible for any human to contain, but only for a short period of time.

I write this to bottle the motivation of death and carry it with me, written down, and so be able to do anything.

The dream of death is only a quick cheat, a quick glimpse into the eternal; though I can feel now the angels pull back from my mind the divine meaning of life and death.

They scold me as a young child gotten into something only for grown-ups. So that now I write after something I've lost.

Earthquake cont.

If only I could remember the dread of falling into the great crack of an earthquake, and so then muster all the life left in me.

Alas, try as I might—laying up in bed at 4:35 a.m.—it is an emotion beyond words—such a sense of gratitude bore by death.

Because it is only for one person to experience one time what it means to really lose everything all at once.

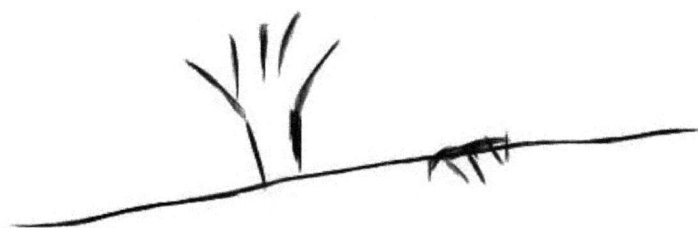

"That's very well said, and may all be true, but let's cultivate our garden."

- Candide to Dr. Pangloss

REFERENCES

Page

46   Sartre, Jean-Paul. *Nausea.*

46   Nietzsche, Friedrich. *Thus Spake Zarathustra.*

59   Chesterton, G. K. *Orthodoxy.*

62   Sartre, Jean-Paul. "Existentialism Is a Humanism."

88   Camus, Albert. *The Plague.*